CHINA EXPOSED!!

BY CHE S CHIBALA

"Then I stood on the sand of the sea and behold, a great, fiery red dragon rose up out of the sea, having seven heads and ten horns. His tail drew a third of the stars of heaven and threw them to the earth." Blessed is he who reads and those who hear the words of this prophecy; for the time is near, things that must surely take place.

CHAPTER ONE

China is the largest of all Asian countries with vast landscape encompassing grassland, desert, mountains, lakes, rivers and more than 14,000km of coastline. Its capital, Beijing mixes modern architecture with historic sites such as the Forbidden City palace complex and Tiananmen Square. Shanghai is a skyscraper-studded global financial center. The iconic Great Wall of China runs east-west across the country's north and has the largest population in the world of any other country in the world. It covers an area of 9,560,900 square kilometers, which is approximately one fourteenth of the land area of the world; among the major countries of the world it is surpassed in area only by Russia and Canada, and it is larger than either the United States or Brazil. Its population officially estimated to number about one and a half billion represents a fifth of the world's population; statistically speaking there is one Chinese for every four persons of other nationality. Both in area and population, Europe excluding Russia is only half the size of Chuna. In general terms, a Chinese province may thus be equal to a country in Europe. The

Chinese province of Kiangsi, for example, while only one third of Sweden has more than triple Sweden's population, while the province of Kiangsu, with only one fifth the area of Spain, has nearly one and half times Spain's population. The People's Republic of Chuna, a country in East Asia, stretches for about 5, 000 kilometers from east to west and about 5, 500 kilometers from north to south. In the early 1970's China had twenty nine administrative units directly under the central government, these consisted of twenty one provinces, five autonomous regions and three municipalities.

With more than four thousand years f recorded history, China is one of the few existing countries that also flourished economically and culturally in the earliest stage of world civilization. In the century preceding 1950, however, it experienced an era of dire anarchy and decrepitude. Under regimes that often proved to be inefficient and corrupt, it remained helpless as foreign powers nibbled at the territory and as its humiliated people struggled for bare subsistence. Although it was called "an independent" country its status and condition resembled that of a foreign colony. A revolution occurred after the end of the Second World War, it was a cataclysm that changed China overnight. The establishment of the Communist government in China in 1949 marked the beginning of a new era and created a new pattern of political geography. By the early 1970's, Chuna had developed into a super power, unchallenged as one of the three most influential countries in the world.

Since the 1980s, China's Communist Party has been using "socialist market economy" to describe their nation's economic system. China's economy is subject to market forces, and capitalists are involved, but the Party does not believe that capitalists run their economy. It is the world's largest emerging market economy, both in terms of population and total economic product. The country is arguably the world's most important manufacturer and industrial producer, and those two sectors alone account for more than 40% of China's gross domestic product, or GDP.

The socialist market economy of the People's Republic of China is the world's second largest economy by nominal GDP and the world's largest economy by

purchasing power parity. Until 2015, China was
the world's fastest-growing major economy, with growth rates averaging 10% over 30 years. This growth rate is now estimated to be the same for global influence rate in all fields.

We should not be surprised if the Chinese Yuan takes over the United States dollar as a global trading currency. If 1.4 billion Chinese who are very productive, dynamic and wealthy might just decide that anyone trading with them must use the Chinese currency rather than the US dollar. Why should they use the US dollar? They are the people with the money, property with the wealth. So one day they will decide that if you want to buy, you have to use the Chinese currency. And you will have no choice; you will have to use Chinese currency. I don't know how long we can resist, but it will come one day. Such a move will definitely displease the United States of America which will go bankrupt if the US dollar is no longer used as the world's trading currency.

At one time an ounce of gold was the equivalent of US$36, but today the price is US$1,200, forcing America to go off the gold standard while "maintaining the fiction that it carries the same value. Now one ounce of gold is about US$1,200. That's how much the US dollar has depreciated but we have been brought up to think of the US dollar as the standard. Other currencies too can be the standard but the US will feel very unhappy if you drop the dollar as the standard for currencies. If you don't use the US dollar, the US will go bankrupt immediately because it owes the world 14 trillion dollars which they cannot pay. They don't have that much gold to pay. So if you switch from US to the Chinese currency, the US is going to feel very unhappy.

CHAPTER TWO

The Chinese People's Liberation Army is the armed forces of the People's Republic of China and Communist Party of China. The PLA consists of five professional service branches: the Ground Force, Navy, Air Force, Rocket Force, and the Strategic Support Force. The People's Liberation Army Ground Forces is the largest army in Asia. Numbering 1.6 million active duty troops, the PLAGF is charged with securing China's borders, providing a capability to project land power in China's neighborhood and increasingly, on a global scale.

The Chinese army is one of the five most powerful armies on earth; with a soldier population is estimated to be 7,054,000 in total, while the American army consists of less than 3 million soldiers. Obviously, Chinese can staff more men in a potent fight with USA.

Every year, as part of its annual state budget, China releases a single overall figure for national military expenditures. For example in 2016, the Chinese government's official defense spending figure was $146 billion, an increase of 11% from the budget of$131 billion in 2014. Chinese military spending is only surpassed by the United States which has a budget of around $612.5 billion. With the second largest defense spending in the world, which rose to over $150 billion in 2017, China is rapidly modernizing its army and could soon pose serious challenges to US military dominance.

China has made impressive strides in a number of key areas that it sees as crucial to deterring potential adversaries and, if necessary, winning future wars. Experts point out that the efforts to modernize the army show that China understands how the realm of modern warfare has changed. China is preparing its capabilities for potential conflict that may take place in the sea, air, cyber and space domains.

China opened its first overseas naval base in Djibouti, located 6,688 km from China, a small nation in the Horn of Africa, on August 1, 2017, signaling

Beijing's intention to project its military power beyond the Asia Pacific. This is just one example of the projects being used to advance China's national security interests.

These investments are already generating political influence, stealthily expanding China's military presence, and creating an advantageous strategic environment in the region.
Strategic investments in the 15 ports across the Indo-Pacific region reflect China's ambition to become a rising maritime power. China could potentially establish a few more bases in the next few years to expand its naval influence beyond its neighboring

regions. As China continues its efforts to modernize its army and expand its military influence, Beijing is posing both direct and indirect challenges to the US, and the world at large. There is a clear action-reaction dynamic between Beijing and Washington in the military realm.

While the Indian Ocean, Middle East and Africa remain the regional priorities for China, Beijing has also deployed naval vessels to the Mediterranean and Baltic Seas, reflecting its growing military capabilities and ambition. The increasing regularity of these deployments is an indicator of China's growing confidence and ambition.

In closing a nationalistic speech to parliament, president Xi Jinping, where laid out China's vision, he promised of a new era of military might. Xi said that any nation interfering in China's territorial integrity would face "the punishment of history."

CHAPTER THREE

A new global rich list tallied 104 billionaires in the upper echelons of China's leadership. China minted206 billionaires in the 2017, taking the country's total to 819 billionaires 40% more billionaires than in the US. There were 1.34 million millionaires in China in 2016, an increased from 1.21 million in the previous year. This in line with the part's vision as outlined by President Xi Jinping, when he declared that

China has entered a "new era," and his plan to restore the country to global prominence is clear: Just as the Chinese Communist Party (CCP) controls China's domestic life, it intends to control foreign policy as well and very soon the world.

While the CCP has always controlled the direction of foreign policy, its hand is increasingly visible in foreign-policy implementation: the CCP Central Committee, the center of political power in China, is returning to its own organizational strengths as a Leninist political party to push its interests in the global arena. A recent report compiled by top

American China experts noted this increasingly assertive stance in the United States, but the CCP's efforts are global.

While the party utilizes united front work to unify a diverse set of interest groups to support communist rule, the UFWD is now ramping up its campaign to attract the support of international actors for China's foreign policy.

Examples of the China's global operations are numerous. In Australia, CCP efforts to influence Australian politics through campaign donations where investigated ; in October 2017, UFWD's own teaching manual instructs united-front cadres to target Chinese-Canadian politicians for their operations; and a New Zealand lawmaker revealed that he was instructed by his own party leadership to obscure a donation from a businessman associated with the China, raising the same foreign-influence concerns as those of Australia. Despite these growing revelations, The CCP's self-confidence has led to a united-front counteroffensive instead of a tactical retreat.

Taking the recent example of the 'Belt and Road Initiative' a step taken by China in enhancing the to connect 65

Taking the recent example of the 'Belt and Road Initiative' a step taken by China in enhancing the trade and connectivity of Asia and Africa, it aims to connect 65 countries accounting for over 30% in the global GDP with a 62% of population in the concerned areas and contains 75% of the known energy sources. The 'Belt and Road Initiative' will not only act as means of connectivity, but will simultaneously change the existing trade routes and major trade powers. China has emerged as the largest investor for almost all African countries.

In a message that Chinese officials have been pushing ever since their country's spectacular rise began. Wang Yi, China's foreign minister, said, "China will not, repeat, not repeat the old practice of a strong country seeking hegemony,"

For decades, they have been at pains to downplay China's power and reassure other countries—especially the United States of its benign intentions. Jiang Zemin, China's leader in the 1990s, called for mutual trust, mutual benefit, equality, and cooperation in the country's foreign relations. Under Hu Jintao, who took the reins of power in 2002, "peaceful development" became the phrase of the moment. The current president, Xi Jinping, insists that

China "lacks the gene" that drives great powers to seek hegemony. It is easy to dismiss such protestations as simple deceit. In fact, however, Chinese leaders are telling the truth: Beijing truly does not want to replace Washington at the top of the international system. China has no interest in establishing a web of global alliances, sustaining a far-flung global military presence, sending troops thousands of miles from its borders, leading international institutions that would constrain its own behavior, or spreading its system of government abroad.

But to focus on this reluctance, and the reassuring Chinese statements reflecting it, is a mistake. Although China does not want to usurp the United States' position as the leader of a global order, its actual aim is nearly as consequential. In the Indo-Pacific region, China wants complete dominance; it wants to force the United States out and become the region's unchallenged political, economic, and military hegemon. And globally, even though it is happy to leave the United States in the driver's seat, it wants to be powerful enough to counter Washington when needed, getting to do what they want, and nobody say anything about it. In a speech to the Chinese Communist Party Congress in Beijing's Great Hall of the People, President Xi Jinping said it was time for his nation to transform itself into 'a mighty force' that could lead the entire world on political, economic, military and environmental issues. That's quite an ambition. The Party Congress is basically China's Parliament except that it only meets once every five years and only has one party.

CHAPTER FOUR

China has a problem; its **population** does not match its resources and gross domestic product. China's more than 1.4 billion people don't have the resources to adequately care for themselves. This has led China to begin exporting its people to other parts of the world. Look no further than Africa, where China has rapidly developed its presence during the last decade, in countries like Nigeria and Angola, among others. During that time, more than 750,000 Chinese have moved to Africa. Some experts contend that the plan is to increase this number to the hundreds of millions, helping to put a dent into China's natural resource problem by tapping into Africa's resources, while thinning the herd in the home country. Air and sea routes are increasing between China and African nations as massive deals are made for commodities, trade, labor and military cooperation. Chinese private schools, embassies and cultural centers are popping up in places like Rwanda, Nairobi and Angola. Angola even has its own "Chinatown" district.

In return, countries in Africa get a willing trade partner, assistance and weaponry for its military factions. Africa also receives the supposed benefit of jobs and infrastructure building. While trade has increased from 5 million Yuan to 6 billion, many contend that Africa is getting the short end of the stick, importing cheap Chinese toys and goods, while exporting valuable commodities like oil and timber. It's estimated that 70 percent of African timber ends up in

Chinese ports, a figure that hints at massive deforestation. Chinese mining operations in Africa are staffed with African laborers earning less than one Yuan per day, which is about 14 cents. The weapons sent to Africa often supply arms that help to fuel the continents many civil wars.

Similarly, China has reached out to Latin America as well, bypassing the United States as Brazil's No. 1 trading partner, and coming in second to the United States in Argentina, Costa Rica, Chile, Peru and Venezuela. With this kind of reach, and a population at well over a billion people, it's no wonder that a large percentage of the global financial news focuses on China. But is China poised to become a true superpower?

It doesn't matter how many Friendship Bridges are built, or how many Cooperation Summits are organized. As long as attitudes toward other races and nations do not change within China, the relationships that are cultivated abroad will be exploitative, with only rapacious advancement of one party as a result.

The term coined for the present exploitation is what is called 'neo-colonialism. The essence of neo-colonialism is that the State which is subject to it is, in theory, independent and has all the outward trappings of international sovereignty. In reality, its economic system and political policy is directed from outside. In a much simpler version, neo-colonialism has been defined as another form of colonialism where the present independent state remains dependent on their former colonial masters politically, economically and socially. The context of China and its development has time and again been linked to 'strategies' in capturing areas in the name of 'neo-colonialism'. The debate goes around Chinese investments and foreign aids as a way of being a 'neo-colonial' leader in the African and Asian regions.

Africa has always been under exploitation since the colonial masters realized the value of the territory and also the strategic location. Africa was left with a legacy of imperialism and it became difficult in determining the path towards development and modernization. The path for modernization was and still is chosen through financial aids and assistance from foreign societies. But this constant dependence on foreign countries for aid and the growing power of multinational corporations directs the perspective towards neo-colonialism. The present era of globalization, which undoubtedly have brought world economies closer is now being scrutinized under the light of 'a corridor to neo-colonialism' with cultural subjugation. Africa can be seen locked up in between three dominant world powers; Europe, America and China, of which China has emerged the leader in increasing its home economy by channelizing local African companies to work for China. The value of trade between China and Africa has amounted to $200 billion back in 2014 and the numbers just seem to be ever growing. It has projected to amount to 25% of global power energy but is motivated by Beijing's resource extraction.

Though the states of Africa have attained political freedom, economic and cultural freedom still lies with the world superpower.

China was likely to take over the huge port of Mombasa from the Kenyan government after a near default by Kenya Railways Corporation on loans from the Exim Bank of China. This is possible because Kenya, along with many other nations along China's 'One Belt One Road' project, signed away its sovereign rights to Beijing upon taking billions from China for infrastructure projects. The China Exim bank would have become principal over Kenyan

Port Authority had Kenyan Railways Corporation defaulted in its obligations. This is become a pattern across the developing world. A similar situation recently went down in Sri Lanka where the government lost its Hambantota port to China. Zambia also will lose Kenneth Kaunda International Airport to China over failure of debt repayment.

Asia, another continent which had been a victim of colonialism is now being evaluated on its performance from being free from actual 'colonialism. China is slowly emerging as the dominant economy in the whole South East

Asia. Chinese investments in the last decade have gone up and it is steadily increasing the investments too. In terms of infrastructure, the construction projects are taken by China in the region amounts to $100 million, from $5.68 billion in 2005 to $38.01 billion in 2017. Asia has attracted China mainly for its energy sources. China was criticized for the 'belt and road initiative' as well the development that took place in Sri Lanka when massive lands of the Colombo port were given to Chinese multinationals. This kind of behavior very closely resembles the European colonialism. Beijing is exerting great pressure on local political and cultural dynamics. Also, these investments are putting some countries in debt with Chinese soil and depleting national treasures. These are some facts backed by data which directs towards Chinese neo-colonialism, however, some still argue that such investments should not be viewed under the light of such 'scrutiny. The blame cannot be put on Beijing as these channels help in the internal movement of goods and trade, a positive for any developing country. Moreover, the point of national treasures is tackled as many thinkers have pointed out that the countries aren't forced to sign up for these projects which include massive funds. There has to be a two-way benefit and that's how trade happens in the 21st-century globalized world.

CHAPTER FIVE

About 1 million Chinese citizens have arrived in Africa since 2001, with China emerging as Africa's largest trading partner and Chinese companies stepping up investment in oil and infrastructure projects. Most are workers, traders and entrepreneurs. The communities are scattered from South Africa to Tanzania, Zambia, Ghana, Nigeria, Angola, Mauritius, Madagascar and Algeria. No one knows for sure how many

Chinese live in Africa because of a shortage of reliable statistics from African governments. Estimates range from 250,000 to 2 million.

Zambia has anywhere from 13,000 and 23,000 Chinese nationals, and many arrived in the last several years as workers for Chinese state-owned enterprises or private firms. Chinese investors are heavily invested in local mining operations.

The debate about Chinese neocolonialism is long standing but has re-emerged with new force for two reasons. One is China's 'One Belt, One Road initiative,' which anticipates billions of dollars' worth of infrastructure projects and resource investments in dozens of countries, many economically and politically weak. Indeed, the general features of China's relations with many countries today bear close resemblance to the European colonial powers' relations with African and Middle Eastern countries in the 19th and 20th century. Among other things, we witness countries exchanging their primary products for Chinese manufactured ones; China dominating the local economy; countries becoming heavily indebted to Beijing; China exerting greater weight on local political, cultural and security dynamics. For a number of reasons, Beijing has been at pains to rebut accusations that it is yet another neocolonial power exploiting partners through unequal exchange. It has argued, rightly, that local country shipments of agricultural commodities, coal, gas and oil, and resources like copper, tin and uranium, to China have benefited countries such as Australia, Kazakhstan and Namibia. China also contends that its economic links with its partners have helped them develop by addressing their infrastructure gaps, boosting employment, facilitating industrialization, transferring technology and knowledge, and expanding power generation and distribution capabilities.

Critics offer several counterarguments. Beijing's connectivity infrastructure projects are essentially an initiative to send more resources to China. Chinese projects afford local countries a scant role and that the debts associated with these projects are depleting national treasuries. Chinese projects specifically and investments more generally insufficiently use local suppliers and partners. Chinese companies and projects contribute little to job creation, partly because they use so many Chinese laborers. China is not sharing important technology and is doing more harm than good regarding host country industrialization because its cheap goods destroy local manufacturing. China's slogan of "win-win" essentially means China wins twice. There is no doubt that some Chinese infrastructure projects are about enhancing China's resource security, but many including highways, power distribution lines and railways are not. Indeed, they will facilitate internal exchange of goods, services and peoples. Other projects will integrate countries into global production networks or regional connectivity schemes. And it should be recognized that Chinese constructed airports,

ports and special economic zones are "dual use" in that what goes in and out need not be just from or to China. As for the issue of depleting national treasuries, it is odd to blame this problem on Beijing. China is not forcing countries to accept bad projects or incur debts through pressure or deception about project viability. Furthermore, China is not dispensing "cheap opium" in the form of preferential loans to ensnare countries in a "debt trap."

The problem of Beijing inadequately using local partners and suppliers is a genuine one, but that Chinese companies should automatically use local ones is not ideal if the latter cannot do projects well or supply the needed quality and quantity of goods. Moreover, given the political situation in host countries, local partners and suppliers will be selected because of their political ties, not project implementation abilities. The issue of Chinese job creation is an important one, too, but there are unrealistic expectations about what Chinese investment and contracting can do. For many countries, because of the skill level of their workers, the most promising areas for job creation will be in low-value added areas; that is, not the areas in which China is involved. Moreover, host country workers will have more opportunities when they can do what Chinese companies need, as is the case with companies of all nationalities.

Questioning the sufficiency of technology transfer by Chinese companies also is legitimate. But hammering Chinese firms to do more is not a viable way to redress the problem. Chinese companies are not going to transfer more or better technology unless it is in their interests, as China knows from its own dealings with foreign companies. In addition, technology transfers will not be particularly beneficial until host countries and companies boost their "absorptive capacity." Chinese competition has placed severe pressure on China's economic partners both in the latter's home markets as well as in third-party markets. The challenges seem even more ominous given China's plans to invest more and build Special economic Zones and ports which will allow China to export even more goods to its partners and these partners' partners. Cheap, low quality Chinese goods also permit local firms to remain competitive and improve the access of consumers to a greater range and quantity of goods, and forces local firms to upgrade their competitive abilities. Moreover, in numerous cases, China's economic partners have squandered or not fully employed the gains from their massive commodity sales to China to diversify and improve their industrial competitiveness. Put differently, a complete picture requires us to recognize that cheap Chinese goods also bring benefits and further that host governments have not done all that they could have done to mitigate the China challenge.

Chinese projects, investment, and the 'One Belt, One Road', sarcastically termed "One Belt, One Trap", are supposed to deliver a lot of the first two, and may not be an unvarnished blessing. But their potential upsides may be greater than recognized while the negatives may be exaggerated. Regardless, the maximization or equalization of the net benefits will not occur if the critics expect "win-win" to mean "win-lose", meaning China gives all and gets nothing in return, denigrate all Chinese projects and investment, or belittle all Chinese loans.

For their part, host countries need to improve their ability to bargain with the Chinese side by leveraging other countries and companies, and manipulating market access. They further need to improve the capacities of their firms and workers to maximize employment, technology transfer and partnership opportunities. Rather than just disparaging China, they should contemplate how they can empower host countries.

CHAPTER SIX

China's exploitative relationship abroad with African nations became most evident when it was discovered that the Chinese government's gift of a headquarters building and computer network for the African Union in Addis Ababa contained a back door to facilitate the transfer of data to servers in Shanghai. The myth of Chinese support for African nations has been perpetuated both at home and abroad, with the $200 million AU complex in Addis as the crown jewel within the narrative of international cooperation fostered by Chinese public funds. But the charm in Beijing's Africa blitz doesn't hide the profiteering and wrangling for influence that follow.

China's move into Djibouti is a prime example. The tiny east African nation sits along one of the world's major maritime shipping lanes, and is home to American, French, German, Italian, and Japanese military bases, with the latest addition of a Chinese "logistics and supply center" to the many foreign military installations already there. The Chinese naval facility was inaugurated last summer, and is part of Chinese President Xi Jinping's plan to modernize his country's military, expanding its navy's blue-water capabilities.

Beijing shells out $20 million a year to lease the real estate for its base in Djibouti, and has already stationed over 1,000 troops there, with sufficient space for 10 times that number if needed. On top of that, the Chinese government has given the host nation loans topping $1.1 billion to upgrade its commercial port, build an additional airport, a railway that stretches to Addis Ababa, and a water pipeline that moves water from Ethiopia. Some Djibouti officials have expressed concern about their country's ability to repay those loans; failure to channel funds back to China would place the nation in an undesirable position in the very near future. In Kenya, controversy is unfolding around the country's largest infrastructure project independence. A Chinese-built railway has been designed to be extended through the wildlife reserve just outside of Nairobi. A court ordered that construction be halted as the case is reviewed, but builders and engineers from the China Road and Bridge Corporation have already begun work, with protection from armed guards.

A ranking member of the U.S. Senate Armed Services Committee has already warned of China's influence in African nations. After a recent trip to the region, he said, "Wherever we're going in Africa, they seem to be there, or following close behind." It isn't even clear whether America aims to cooperate with China on the continent, counter its clout, or implement a combination of the two options. Beijing's goals, however, are much clearer. Chinese industrialists often with the state's backing are eyeing their moves to a new continent as the economic and governance models at home switch gears. Ethiopia, for instance, has received a cash injection of nearly $11 billion to bulk up its industrial infrastructure, transforming farmland into industrial parks that can house factories that churn out fast fashion clothing items and consumer electronic goods. The country has opened four such parks since 2014, and plans to launch eight more before 2020. Hundreds of Ethiopian farmers have complained of land grabs, displacement, and lack of compensation, as the government clears space for newcomers from Beijing.

China has embarked on the most ambitious infrastructure project in modern world history. It's called the 'Belt and Road Initiative,' and it spans three continents and covers almost 60 percent of the world's population China plans to become the world's next superpower.

The initiative essentially has two parts, the economic belt, is made up of six corridors that direct trade to and from China. These corridors include roads, railways, bridges, power plants and anything that makes it easier for Europe, Asia, and Africa to trade goods with China. The second part, the maritime Silk Road, is a chain of seaports from the South China Sea to the Indian Ocean that direct maritime trade to and from China.

China is loaning trillions of dollars to countries willing to host these projects. They're promoted as a win-win for everyone. Many of the countries involved need new infrastructure and access to new markets, while China needs new projects for its growing construction industry. But many of the countries involved in the BRI are authoritarian, corrupt, and in conflict risky places for China to invest money in.

CHAPTER SEVEN

Zambia is a classic example of understanding the African-Chinese relation, as even after repeated implantation of labor laws, the country continues to be one of the richest in the African continent. The 'Belt and Road Initiative' is also about to change the face of trade as economists have it, but the entire model needs slight reforms. As for Asia, particularly India the dominance is yet settling in and the aspect of neo-colonialism hasn't yet been properly channelized into view, as most of the countries in Asia are still undergoing major changes in 'state structures.' The whole debate goes on as the concept of neo-colonialism is a new subfield of study, demanding more experiments backed by facts and value.

Zambia's public debt has increased significantly in recent years, and concerns over a possible crisis have lately attracted the attention of Western media. British business intelligence outlet Africa Confidential warned of escalating debt caused by allegedly unsustainable Chinese loans and claimed that the state-owned national electricity company has been in talks about a takeover by a Chinese company. The Zambian government refuted the allegations and denied the existence of plans for company privatization. The allegations coincided with increased Western concern over the expansion of Chinese loans to African countries. Two weeks after the UK froze its aid following an investigation into large-scale corruption in a Social Cash Transfer program it supported; other donors, Ireland, Finland and Sweden, did the same.

In August, 2018 US senators sent a letter to the US Secretaries of Treasury and State, to warn against China's use of "debt-trap diplomacy" to advance the Belt and Road Initiative and create a world economic order centered on the Asian superpower. They wrote that China pumps large loans for infrastructure projects into countries in Africa, Asia and Europe with the explicit purpose of leveraging the debt to influence national policies and gain control over strategic assets and resources. They expressed concern over the role of the International Monetary Fund in bailing out countries indebted to China and called for decisive action to stop the Chinese "hegemonic" project.

However, the reality of Zambia's debt tells a different story: China is not the only major player. China probably holds a quarter to a third of Zambia's external debt. In recent years, Zambia joined several other African countries in borrowing US dollars through large bond sales on international markets controlled by Western institutions. The government issued three Eurobonds for a total of $3billion; this does not include interest repayments, which keep going up. The yields on these bonds have reached 17 percent. The first 10-year Eurobond was issued in 2012 with a 5.6 percent yield. It is also true that Zambia has heavily borrowed from Chinese sources and critics point out that a large number of these loans might be unaccounted for in the government official figures. Either way, the government declared a staggering $9.4bn of external debt in 2018 or 34.7 percent of GDP, up from $1.9bn at the end of 2011, or 8.4 percent of GDP. But while the figures are worrying, it is irresponsible to pour fuel on the fire. A debt default would open up opportunities for vulture funds and international creditors to take over the country's rich mineral and land resources and the few remaining parastatals that survived two decades of aggressive privatization and public spending cuts imposed by the IMF and the World Bank from the 1980s to the mid-2000s.

Health, education and other public services have already been decimated and the mining sector, previously under state control, is now for the most part in foreign hands as are most sectors of the formal economy. Zambia is the 4th most unequal country in the world, and 74.3 percent of the population lives on less than $3.20 a day. It is a tragic irony that China is now being blamed by the West for allegedly doing exactly what the IMF has been doing for decades: providing unsustainable loans to countries in need to further plunge them into debt, weaken state capacity and open up national economies to international investors, primarily from Western countries. While China might be pursuing its own debt traps, they are certainly less experienced than the IMF when it comes to leveraging debt over heavily indebted countries. The real story here is not that Zambia is - once again trapped by international creditors. Rather it is that the IMF and its Western allies are scared of losing their grip on Zambia and other African countries, threatened by the parallel economic system that China has built in recent years.

China is understandably hiding details of its loans from IMF oversight and Zambia an open threat to Western hegemony due to leaders' vocal support for Beijing. After protracted negotiations over a failed bailout, the IMF recalled its envoy from Zambia, apparently under pressure from government officials unhappy with his conduct. The Zambian government's blatant mismanagement of public finances and the president's increasingly authoritarian tendencies show that his stance is far from principled and is driven by desperation. But Western criticism of the Zambian president is not well intentioned either. The Western media has downplayed the fact that an eventual IMF bailout would come with hefty conditionalities, imposing further spending cuts and privatizations in an already downsized state. There is no evidence that suggests that an IMF program would be better than a Chinese deal.

It was the IMF and World Bank that pushed hard for the privatization of the national electricity company in the 1990s and early 2000s. The company became a symbol of resistance in a country that was largely sold out to foreign investors and their local brokers in business and politics. The attempts at privatizing the parastatal failed. In 2016, talks of privatization resurfaced. Throughout 2016, rumors about Saudi Arabia's interest in buying the electricity company circulated in connection with the president's visit to the kingdom.

We should be careful however not to replace one form of xenophobia 'anti-Chinese sentiment', with another. In a world of depleted mineral resources, Western countries, especially resource-dependent, need Zambia's copper, uranium and cobalt - the latter is in high demand recently due to the booming electric vehicle industry. The West is also interested in the landlocked country's strategic position at the heart of the African continent. Zambia has borders with eight countries and close ties with neighboring conflict ridden and resource rich Democratic Republic of the Congo.

Hopefully, the country will not default. If it does, the biggest losers will be the Zambian people. A default could trigger a chain reaction and bring down other African economies that borrowed heavily through Eurobonds and are struggling with debt repayments. What Zambia needs is debt cancellation and a strong state that takes back control of strategic national resources such as mining and agricultural land. Thanks to his nationalization policies, the first president, Kenneth Kaunda, was able to make significant progress on reverting Zambia's colonial legacy and redistributing national wealth across society. With all the neoliberal rhetoric that has dominated Zambian politics in the past three decades, many Zambians look back with nostalgia at those years. However, the current President is not willing or able to deliver wide-ranging redistributive reforms of the kind implemented by Kaunda. Zambians will have to search elsewhere if they hope to revert the trend.

A major worry of the IMF and US is that China's Belt and road strategy is first to encourage indebtedness, and then to take over strategic national assets when debtors default on repayments. The state-owned TV and radio news channel is already Chinese-owned. The long-term outcome could be effective Chinese ownership of the commanding heights of the economy and potentially the biggest loss of national sovereignty since independence; Zambians would be alarmed to learn the real Chinese debt figures. Zambia is a good example of what the International Monetary Fund and the United States Senate are calling a crisis of accelerating developing-country indebtedness to China. In a bipartisan letter by prominent US Senators to US Treasury Secretary urged the US not to allow the IMF to bail out countries which had got themselves into financial difficulties thanks to over-exposure to Chinese debt, especially for 'overpriced' infrastructure projects. The Senators' letter names 'predatory Chinese infrastructure financing' as part of 'debt-trap diplomacy' which is integral to the Belt Road Initiative. The letter continues that Twenty three of the 68 developing countries are in debt distress or strong risk thereof because of the Belt Road Initiative.

Although Zambia is classified as at high risk of debt distress it is not among the 23 named, but is only because much of its debt to China has not been fully accounted for, an exercise the Lusaka exchequer is not anxious to complete for fear of the alarm the figures would cause. The Zambian government is supposed to be contributing 15% of its own money to the Chinese financed projects. Meeting this commitment is testing government finances to the limit and taking precedence over social expenditure. Although the Finance Minister announced that all projects below 80 per cent completion would be halted, the president publicly assured Chinese nationals that all projects would go ahead as planned there would be 'no disruption in the ongoing projects' financed by China. Since the current president came to power, Zambia has signed off on at least US$8 billion in Chinese project finance. Over $5 billion of this has not been added to the total because Zambia insists the money has not been disbursed, and more large loans are in the pipeline. Yet the finance ministry does not have the capacity, to police, let alone stem, all the spending. In some cases, the financial penalties for halting disbursement on projects would outweigh the savings. Donor governments have offered technical assistance to bring the project debt mountain under control but have been rebuffed. An IMF representative was asked to leave on accusations that he was spreading negative talk. The debt continues to spiral and the role of Chinese projects in it raises more concern. Having allocated US$500 million to external debt service this year, the government's liquidity crisis drags on as relations with donors and international financial institutions plummet. Lusaka asked the International Monetary Fund to withdraw its resident representative on the grounds that he was supposedly 'spreading negative talk' among the donors, a source in Lusaka said. The rift is a blow to any chance – practically non-existent though it already was of a deal.

Britain's Department for International Development was investigating three ministries for fraud.
Financial management across the ministries is under scrutiny. Britain's Department for International Development is investigating fraud in three ministries, which could have serious implications for future funding, And Zambian exposure to Chinese debt, especially project credit, is still causing concern. Meanwhile, Government

had continued spending lavishly despite the country being in debt distress.

In mid-July 2018 Lusaka announced a supplementary budget of 7.2 billion kwacha ($721 million). Half of this for debt service, which leaves only just enough for public sector salaries, which it is struggling to pay. Efforts to raise capital domestically are not going well. The auctions of Treasury Bills have been poorly subscribed on average although it has been using massive inducements to attract the banks. Government data shows that by the end of May 2028, it had spent $489 million on external debt service and in July it announced a further

$161.3 million was paid in June. It will need a further $360 million over and above the sum originally budgeted to cover debt service. Domestic measures now in train to re-allocate spending are not realistic and that at least another $300 million needs to come from fresh borrowing.

Critics say Lusaka is hiding the extent of the country's borrowings from Beijing and could be about to hand over control of key state assets. "China equals Hitler", read a poster held up in the Zambian capital Lusaka by a protester opposed to Beijing's tightening grip on the economy of the southern African nation. But he is not alone in opposing China's growing presence in Zambia and, in particular, its major program of loans to Lusaka. In fact his criticism echoes concerns shared by many across swathes of Africa and beyond, where some fear that China's mega projects risk leaving already fragile economies in even worse shape. China is the main investor in Zambia as it is in several other African countries and, with its offers of "unconditional" aid; most public tenders are awarded to Chinese bidders. China is busy building airports, roads, factories and police stations with the boom largely funded by Chinese loans. China is about to take everything from Zambia. They have taken over the economy through these criminal debts. The government is contracting debts from China even without parliamentary approval. Zambian public debt is around US$10.6 billion but that the government is hiding its indebtedness as happened in neighboring Mozambique, which in 2016 was forced to admit it had kept secret US$2 billion of borrowing. Fearing that Zambia might be in a similar position, the International Monetary Fund at one point delayed talks over a US$1.3 billion loan deal. The slump in the price of copper, Zambia's leading export, has led to fears that Lusaka might even struggle to service its existing debt. The state is on the verge of handing control of the national electricity company, Lusaka airport and the state broadcaster to China. Stung by the criticism that he was selling out to China the president hit back at critics say, "I implore you to ignore the misleading headlines that seek to malign our relationship with China by mischaracterizing our economic cooperation to mean colonialism."

CHAPTER EIGHT

It makes clear that the China's goal of building a strong military in the new era is to build the people's forces into world-class forces that obey the Party's command, can fight and win, and maintain excellent conduct. It makes clear that major country diplomacy with Chinese characteristics aims to foster a new type of international relations and build a community with a shared future for mankind. And central to this is what Xi calls "The Thought". The other troubling thing is that the Chinese probably have a window of about five years to 10 years to achieve world domination before they collapse under the weight of their own ageing population. As the tectonic plates of global politics shift, it is worth asking do we want the world to be led by a nation whose guiding principle is this:

"We should not just mechanically copy the political systems of other countries. The CPC stresses the unity of Party leadership, the people running the country, and law-based governance. Party leadership is the fundamental guarantee for ensuring that the people run the country and governance in China is law based; that the people run the country is an essential feature of socialist democracy; and law-based governance is the basic way for the Party to lead the people in governing the country. The system of people's congresses must be upheld and improved to ensure the people's exercise of state power."

Or this:

"We hold these truths to be self-evident: that all men are created equal; that they are endowed by their creator with certain unalienable rights; that among these are life, liberty and the pursuit of happiness."

But China's relations with Africa, while vast and expanding are undermined by cultural and sometimes rather extraordinary political insensitivity. A recent Chinese action films set in African nations tells the story of a Chinese soldier-turned-mercenary who defeats Somali pirates in underwater combat, and protects aid workers and Chinese nationals from rebels and arms dealers and another film, loosely based on the peaceful evacuation of 600 Chinese nationals from Yemen during the early days of the ongoing war there, but with the addition of gunfights and explosions galore. Both films have lavish action sequences. Both were massive commercial successes. The former is the highest-grossing Chinese film ever. With the archetype of the Chinese Savior firmly established, attitudes within China are showing a lack of racial sensitivity at best and a sense of superiority over other races at worst. In an infamous incident during the Chinese New Year break, a gala show on state television included a skit that involved an Asian woman in blackface and oversized butt pads and an African actor in a monkey suit. Criticisms of the skit were censored. In 2016, an advertisement for a laundry product showed a black man being shoved into a washing machine, only to emerge as a boyish-looking Asian man with skin of a much lighter hue.

Moving off screen, we can see those attitudes play out in Guangzhou's Little Africa, derogatively called "Chocolate City" by locals. Once a vibrant hub where traders from African nations gathered or even settled, the neighborhood has been "beautified" by the city government: street markets that once were abuzz with commerce and camaraderie have been banned; the police maintain a constant presence, checking the passports and visas of the foreigners they encounter; locals often hold the mistaken belief that these outsiders are involved with drug trafficking or prostitution. Many shops have been shuttered. Although Little Africa was once estimated to be the temporary home of over 100,000 people, few Africans walk its streets now. Sections of the once culturally diverse neighborhood have been paved over to build parking lots and erect pristine residential units; often, the new landlords will not allow Africans to sign a lease. A decade ago local authorities were "extremely concerned about the high degree of concentration of Africans into a few Guangzhou neighborhoods. The many entrepreneurs who sought their fortunes by obtaining cheap, sometimes fake, goods in the Pearl River Delta region and shipping them home have been displaced. Even those who have Chinese nationals as spouses aren't guaranteed the right to remain in the country with the families they have built.

But as Chinese state owned conglomerates enter the continent; Africans in China face incessant police raids, harassment, and racist attitudes. Even if they once saw China's rise as a model to emulate, and came to trade, learn, and grow, a flight back home now seems like the only option.

CHAPTER NINE

The Chinese may be increasing their influence, but I urge African countries and leaders to note the following about this angel they don't know;

The Chinese legal system is almost nonexistent which means that if you do investment there you are not protected. That's why most Chinese companies invest short term. If you don't trust the legal system you don't invest long term. Corruption is endemic and it creates an environment that does not reward the best players and does not reward quality. If you do business in China, human relationships are more important than the product you deliver. Education produces people that are good to execute things efficiently but it does not foster independent thinking. Moreover people tend to work to get a situation and not because of interest in the subject matter. It's very difficult to find good innovators and engineers there. They do exist but are rare. While China is surely a great nation and has made amazing progress in the last 30 years, they are probably far from ruling the world; the worst danger for China believes they can rule the world now.

CONTENTS:

The views expressed in this book are the authors' own and only reflect his perspective

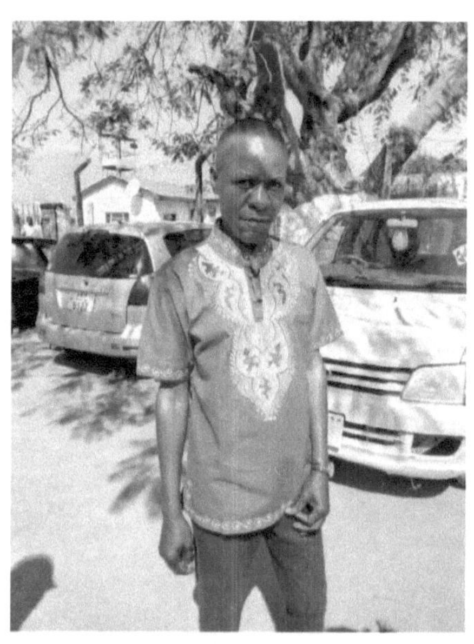

Che S Chibala: He lives in Zambia, Southern Africa and has three daughters. He is a strong animal and climate change advocate who sees so much beauty and goodness in all of nature.

If you enjoyed this book or found it useful I'd be very grateful if you'd post a short review on Amazon. Your support really does make a difference and I read all the reviews personally so I can get your feedback and make this book even better.

Thanks again for your support!

sukanzila1974@gmail.com
sukanzila.blogspot.com
Face book page: "True African adventures"